★ THE NEXT GOAT

CONNOR McDAVID

CORINA JEFFRIES

PowerKiDS press

Published in 2025 by The Rosen Publishing Group, Inc.
2544 Clinton Street, Buffalo, NY 14224

Copyright © 2025 by The Rosen Publishing Group, Inc.

All rights reserved. No part of this book may be reproduced in any form without permission in writing from the publisher, except by a reviewer.

First Edition

Editor: Greg Roza
Book Design: Rachel Rising

Photo Credits: Cover, 9 ZUMA Press, Inc./Alamy Stock Photo; Cover, pp. 1, 3, 4, 6, 8, 10, 12, 14, 16, 18, 20, 22, 23, 24 Pixacon/Shutterstock.com; Cover Farhanz9/Shutterstock.com; Cover, p. 1 Alhovik/Shutterstock.com, p. 4 https://commons.wikimedia.org/wiki/File:Maurice_richard.gif; p. 5 GLYPHstock/Shutterstock.com, p. 7 Ginis Ivuskans/Shutterstock.com; pg. Edmonton_Oilers.jpg; p. 6 GLYPHstock/commons.wikimedia.org/wiki/File:Connor_McDavid_of_the_Edmonton_Oilers.jpg; p. 10 Shell 14/Shutterstock.com; p. 11 https://commons.wikimedia.org/wiki/File:McDavid_sweater.jpg; p. 13 dpa picture alliance/Alamy Stock Photo; pp. 15, 17, 19, 21 ASSOCIATED PRESS/AP Images; p. 16 Ridex Official/Shutterstock.com.

Library of Congress Cataloging-in-Publication Data

Names: Jeffries, Corina, author.
Title: Connor McDavid / Corina Jeffries.
Description: Buffalo : PowerKids Press, [2025] | Series: The next GOAT | Includes index.
Identifiers: LCCN 2024034269 (print) | LCCN 2024034270 (ebook) | ISBN 9781499449730 (lib. bdg.) | ISBN 9781499449723 (paperback) | ISBN 9781499449747 (ebook)
Subjects: LCSH: McDavid, Connor, 1997—Juvenile literature. | Hockey players—Canada—Biography—Juvenile literature. | Edmonton Oilers (Hockey team)—Juvenile literature. | Hockey—Canada—Edmonton—History—Juvenile literature.
Classification: LCC GV848.5.M395 J44 2025 (print) | LCC GV848.5.M395 (ebook) | DDC 796.962092 [B]—dc23/eng/20240812
LC record available at https://lccn.loc.gov/2024034269
LC ebook record available at https://lccn.loc.gov/2024034270

Manufactured in the United States of America

Some of the images in this book illustrate individuals who are models. The depictions do not imply actual situations or events.

CPSIA Compliance Information: Batch #CWPK25. For further information contact Rosen Publishing at 1-800-237-9932.

Find us on

CONTENTS

MEET CONNOR!.	4
EARLY LIFE	6
MINOR LEAGUE HOCKEY.	8
THE ERIE OTTERS	10
TEAM CANADA	12
THE EDMONTON OILERS	14
2024 STANLEY CUP FINALS	18
WHAT'S NEXT?	20
GLOSSARY.	22
FOR MORE INFORMATION	23
INDEX	24

MEET CONNOR!

ROCKET RICHARD TROPHY

Connor McDavid has been a fan favorite in the National Hockey League (NHL) ever since the Edmonton Oilers **drafted** him first overall in 2015. He's won the Art Ross trophy (award) for scoring the most points during the regular season five times. He has won the Hart Memorial Trophy three times as the most **valuable** player in the NHL. These are just two of the awards he's won. With his many successes, many people think McDavid is just a Stanley Cup away from being the next GOAT.

In 2023, McDavid earned the Rocket Richard Trophy for scoring the most goals of the season (64) in the NHL.

EARLY LIFE

Connor McDavid was born on January 13, 1997. He lived outside Toronto, Ontario, and grew up watching the Toronto Maple Leafs. He has an older brother named Cameron McDavid. Connor began skating when he was three. He began playing hockey at four! His parents, Kelly McDavid and Brian McDavid, realized that he was a natural hockey player. When he was just six, Connor began playing in a local league with nine year olds—where he was often the best player on the ice.

Connor McDavid likes to drive young fans to follow their own dreams.

MINOR LEAGUE HOCKEY

As McDavid grew taller and more skillful, he moved up to more **competitive** leagues. He played for the York Simcoe Express, a team in the Ontario Minor Hockey Association (OMHA). His father was the team coach for four years. The team won the OMHA **championship** all four years.

McDavid also played for the Toronto Marlboros, a team in the Greater Toronto Hockey League (GTHL). In his final year with the "Marlies," McDavid scored 33 goals, had 39 **assists**, and earned the title of GTHL Player of the Year.

WHAT THEY'RE SAYING

Sam Gagner, a longtime Oilers player, once trained with McDavid when the then-14-year-old was with the Marlboros. He had this to say to player agent Jeff Jackson: "You gotta find this kid. His name is David O'Connor or something, and he plays for the Marlboros. He's doing things I can't do out there."

In 2015, McDavid attended the Much Music Video Awards in Toronto, Ontario.

THE ERIE OTTERS

When he was 15, McDavid was given "exceptional player **status**." This allows really good players under 16 to play in the Ontario Hockey League (OHL). McDavid was just the third player in history to receive this honor.

The Erie Otters drafted McDavid first overall! He might have been the youngest player in the league, but he quickly showed off his natural talent. The league named him OHL Rookie of the Year. (Rookie means first-year player.) In three seasons, McDavid scored 285 regular season goals, and 68 playoff goals.

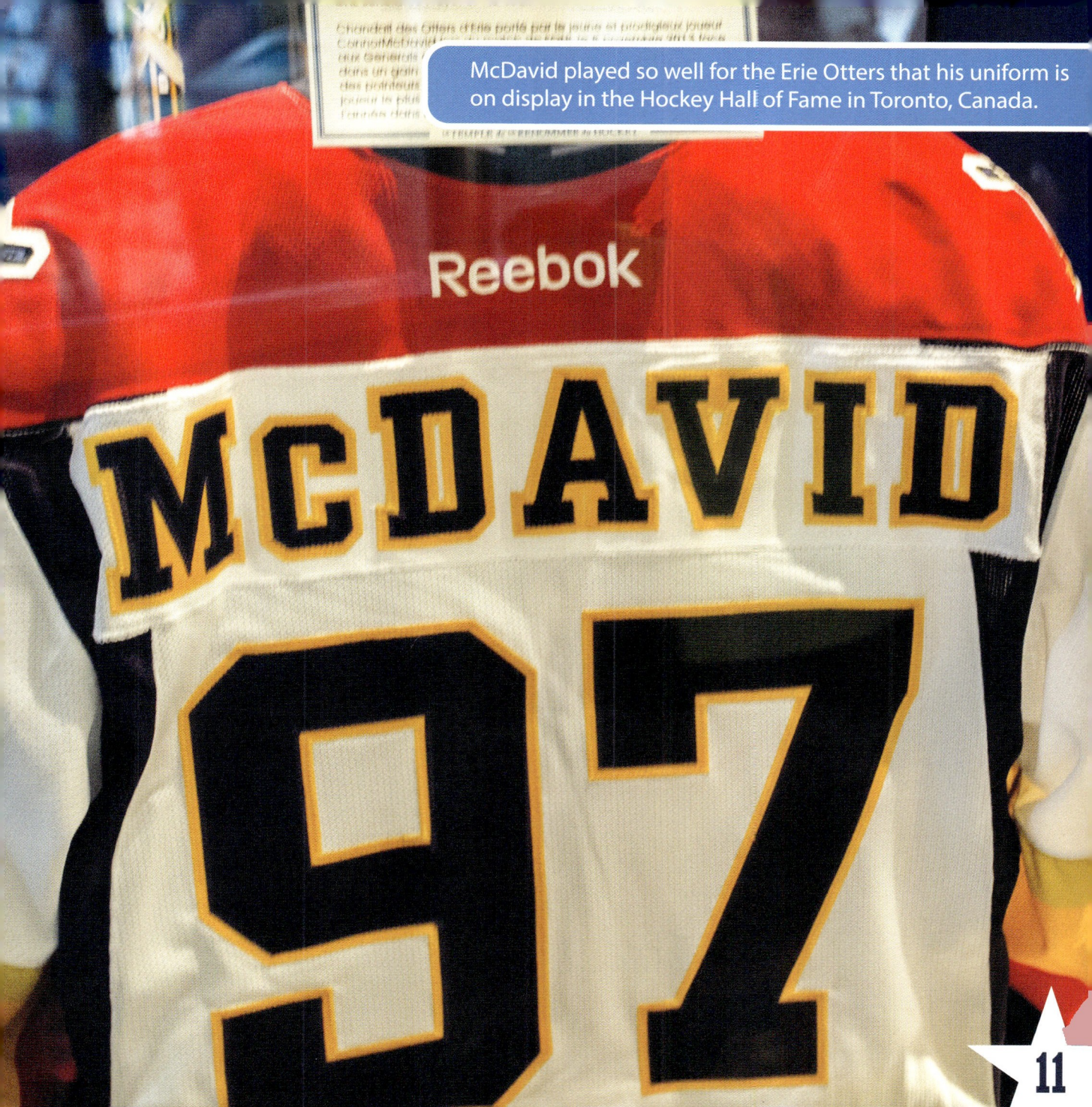

McDavid played so well for the Erie Otters that his uniform is on display in the Hockey Hall of Fame in Toronto, Canada.

TEAM CANADA

McDavid has played for Canada in several **tournaments**. His first was playing at the 2013 International Ice Hockey Federation (IIHF) Under-18 Championship, where the team won a gold medal (first prize). In addition, McDavid was named most valuable player for the tournament.

McDavid played for Canada in the IIHF World Junior Championship in 2014 and 2015. They won the gold medal in 2015. In 2016, McDavid played for Canada in the IIHF World Hockey Championship. Once again, Team Canada won the gold medal!

WHAT THEY'RE SAYING

"It's always been a dream of mine to play at the Olympics since I was a little kid. So, to have that kind of squashed [canceled] as we were getting close was disappointing [sad]."

—**Connor McDavid**

McDavid has said it's a dream of his to play in the Olympics. However, in 2022, the NHL didn't allow players to attend the Olympic games due to COVID-19. His next chance is in 2026.

THE EDMONTON OILERS

McDavid entered the NHL Draft in 2015. Many people talked about him and compared him to other Canadian greats, such as Wayne Gretzky, Mario Lemieux, and Sidney Crosby, all of whom became superstars.

The Edmonton Oilers had the first pick in the draft, and they took McDavid first overall. Unfortunately, McDavid didn't play a full season due to an **injury**. Still, he scored 48 points in 45 games and finished third in the voting for NHL Rookie of the Year.

★ WHAT THEY'RE SAYING

"My initial impression [thoughts] of Connor? 'Wow.' There's no other way to put it."

—Todd McLellan, Edmonton Oilers coach (2015–2019)

For his rookie year, McDavid finished third in voting for the Calder Memorial Trophy (NHL's top rookie) even though he missed 37 games.

15

McDavid received a special honor in 2016. At 19 years old, he became the youngest captain in NHL history. That season he reached 100 points. He helped the Oilers reach the playoffs for the first time since 2006. Although the Oilers lost in the first round, the team gave McDavid an eight-year contract **extension** worth $100 million!

For the 2017–2018 season, McDavid led the NHL with 108 points. He won his second Art Ross Trophy. However, the Oilers failed to make the playoffs.

This is a photograph from McDavid's second year with the Oilers. The letter C on his uniform shows that he's team captain.

2024 STANLEY CUP FINALS

The Oilers made the playoffs every season between 2019 and 2023. For the 2023–2024 season, they made it to the Stanley Cup Finals against the Florida Panthers.

The Oilers lost the first three games (out of seven). However, McDavid led his teammates to win the next three games! Florida won game 7 to become the champs. However, McDavid was voted the most valuable player of the playoffs! He's just the sixth valuable player of a losing team to earn that honor since 1965.

WHAT THEY'RE SAYING

"His ability to create time and space with his speed is something we haven't seen before. It... sets him apart from the rest."

—Edmonton Oilers great Mark Messier

For the 2023–2024 season, McDavid became the fourth player ever to get 100 assists in a single season. Wayne Gretzky did it 11 times. Bobby Orr and Mario Lemieux each did it once. That's pretty good company!

WHAT'S NEXT?

McDavid likes to give back to his community. In 2018, shortly after moving to Edmonton, McDavid raised money to help thousands of Indigenous (Native) youth play sports. He even made time to play floor hockey with them! McDavid also helped set up a shuttle program to drive sick children to doctor's appointments.

Whether he is scoring goals, assisting teammates, or helping the community, Connor McDavid has made a lasting mark on others. Will he be the next NHL GOAT? Many fans say yes!

WHAT THEY'RE SAYING

"Sport has given me so much, and I'm so [thankful] to be able to pay it forward to the next **generation**. This is a community that I'm proud to play for and give back to."

—**Connor McDavid**

20

After the 2022–2023 season, McDavid earned 4 awards. Shown here are the Rocket Richard and Art Ross trophies. He also won the Ted Lindsey Award (for most outstanding player in the regular season) and the Hart Memorial Trophy (for being MVP of his team).

GLOSSARY

assist: In sports, when a player passes the ball or puck to a teammate, who then scores points. Also, to help others.

championship: A contest to find out who's the best player or team in a sport.

competitive: Having a strong desire to win or be the best at something.

draft: A process of selecting young players to be members of the teams in a league.

extension: An increase in the time allowed for something.

generation: All of the people born and living at about the same time.

injury: Harm to the body.

status: Position or rank in relation to others.

tournament: A contest or series of contests played for a championship.

valuable: Important.

FOR MORE INFORMATION

BOOKS

Coleman, Ted. *Edmonton Oilers*. Press Box Books, Mendota Heights, 2023.

Kelley, K. C. *Connor McDavid vs. Mario Lemieux: Who Would Win?* Minneapolis, MN: Learner Publication, 2024.

Stabler, David. *Meet Connor McDavid: Edmonton Oilers Superstar*. Minneapolis, MN: Learner Publications, 2024.

WEBSITES

Kiddle: Connor McDavid Facts for Kids
kids.kiddle.co/Connor_McDavid
Learn more about NHL's next GOAT at this website.

Edmonton Oilers
www.nhl.com/oilers
Keep up with the Oilers at the team's official website.

Publisher's note to educators and parents: Our editors have carefully reviewed these websites to ensure that they are suitable for students. Many websites change frequently, however, and we cannot guarantee that a site's future contents will continue to meet our high standards of quality and educational value. Be advised that students should be closely supervised whenever they access the internet.

INDEX

A
awards/trophies, 4, 5, 8, 10, 12, 16, 18, 21

E
Edmonton Oilers, 4, 8, 14, 15, 16, 17
Erie Otters, 10, 11

G
Gagner, Sam, 8

I
IIHF, 12

M
Mclellan, Todd, 14
Messier, Mark, 18

N
NHL, 4, 5, 13, 16, 20

O
Olympics, 12, 13
OHL, 10
OMHA, 8

P
playoffs, 16, 18

T
Toronto Marlboros, 8

Y
York Simcoe Express, 8